WILLIAM WARREN

By Will Antell

DILLON PRESS, INC.
MINNEAPOLIS, MINNESOTA

Dillon Press, Inc., 500 South Third Street
Minneapolis, Minnesota 55415

Printed in the United States of America

Library of Congress Cataloging in Publication Data

Antell, Will.
    William Warren.

    (The story of an American Indian)
    SUMMARY: A biography of the Ojibway historian
who was the only Indian representative elected to
the Legislature of the Territory of Minnesota in
1850.
        1. Warren, William Whipple, 1825-1853—Juvenile
literature. 2. Chippewa Indians—Juvenile literature.
[1. Warren, William Whipple, 1825-1853.
2. Chippewa Indians—Biography. 3. Indians of
North America—Biography] I. Title.
E99.C6A47   970.3 [B] [92]   72-91157
ISBN 0-87518-056-6

WILLIAM WARREN

Although he led what now must be regarded as an
extraordinary life, William Warren is a little-known
figure in history. The son of an American fur trader
and a mother of French and Ojibway descent, he was
born in 1825 on an island in Lake Superior. Later he
attended school in New York before returning to
Ojibway land to serve as an interpreter and go-between
for government agents and the Ojibways. In 1850, he
was elected to the Minnesota Territorial Legislature —
at a time when Indians were not even allowed to vote.
During the next years, William wrote the *History of the
Ojibways,* based on his knowledge of tribal customs and
legends learned from the elders over lodge fires.
His book was published in 1855, after William Warren's
death by lung disease at the age of twenty-eight.

Contents

FOREWORD

My knowledge of Uncle William is limited to the content of his *History of the Ojibways* and the dimly recalled remarks of his sisters Julia, Mary, and Sophia which I, as a teen-age nephew and grandson, was privileged to hear some forty years ago and shortly before the deaths of these aged ladies.

That I failed to record the wealth of material which these alert women could have provided is due, I suppose, to youthful indifference to history and a concurrent ignorance of the value of these last links with the primitive Ojibways in general and Uncle William in particular.

Despite a lack of written detail, there is an awareness throughout the numerous Warren Clan that Uncle William was indeed a remarkable man. It is known that he died at age twenty-eight after being elected to the Territorial Legislature in 1850, before Indians were permitted to vote. During this brief period from 1850 to his death in 1853, and in spite of failing health, he wrote his *History of the Ojibways* and achieved a position of complete trust and respect in the turbulent Indian and non-Indian communities of his time.

If one were permitted just one word to describe William Whipple Warren, that word would be "dedication"—an obsessive dedication to the well-being of the people of his race and the preservation of their traditions and philosophies which, even then, were fast being buried forever in the graves of the patriarchs.

JAMES (WARREN) HULL

James Hull, grandnephew of William Whipple Warren, is the grandson of Sophia Warren, William's sister. He is a member of the Minnesota Chippewa Tribe, Mississippi Band, and has been living in Grand Portage, Minnesota, since 1953, where he is a trader and business manager for the Grand Portage Band of Chippewa Indians. As the latest in a long line of Cadottes and Warrens to live and work with the Indians of Lake Superior, James Hull hopes that his efforts on behalf of his people will be beneficial to the Chippewas of today, as William Warren's endeavors were to the Indians of his time.

This photograph, from History of the Ojibways, *is the only known picture of William Warren.*

CHAPTER I

A True Son
of the Crane Family

It is impossible to understand Indian history by looking at the shape of a moccasin. An arrowhead found on a lonely beach will not give you a true picture of Indian life. You will not know the real feelings of an Indian by riding in a birch bark canoe. There is an old saying that to truly understand another man you must "walk a mile in his shoes."

Most of the history of the American Indian has been written by white people. Many of these people were fine writers, but it was not possible for them to have a full knowledge of the character and language of the people they were writing about. How fortunate, then, are the Ojibway Indians to have had one of their own people set down the history of their tribe. This man was William Whipple Warren, a descendant of the crane clan of the Ojibways.

In times past the Ojibways were divided into five great clans. Each clan had its own special badge or symbol, called a totem. You have probably heard of totem poles. These were posts that were carved and painted with a series of symbols. Totem poles were placed before a dwelling to represent the ancestors of the people who lived there. The Ojibways called them *nintotem,* which means "my family mark."

The mark of the A-wause clan was the fish totem. The Ah-ah-wauk clan claimed the loon, which is now the state bird of Minnesota. The No-ka clan used the bear as their totem, and the Waub-ish-ash-e clan's totem was the marten.

The crane family, to which William Warren belonged, had the name Bus-in-aus-e, which means "echo-maker." This name was suggested by the loud, clear, and far-sounding cry of the crane, a tall wading bird. The Ojibway people of the crane clan were known for their loud, ringing voices. They also had great skill and power as public speakers. When different tribes held meetings together, members of the crane clan acted as interpreters and expressed the wishes of the tribe.

William Whipple Warren was a true son of the crane family, for he had a marvelous speaking voice that was admired by many people. He often worked as an interpreter, and he represented his people as a member of the Legislature of the Territory of Minnesota. He would also one day write, with great honesty and understanding, the history of his Ojibway people.

William Warren was born on May 27, 1825, at La Pointe Island (later called Madeline Island, in what is now Wisconsin), near the southern shore of the Gitche Gume, which means "a large body of water." William's Gitche Gume was Lake Superior.

The year that William was born the whole Lake Superior country was a clean and beautiful wilderness. The Ojibway Indians were wise enough to do all in their power to protect this beauty, for they knew it was an important part of their lives. They were very careful of the land and of the things that grew from the earth. The tall straight pines, the black and white birch trees, the lakes, streams, soil, and plants were all treated with respect. The Ojibways believed that all this beauty and space had been given to them by the wisdom and love of Gitche Manitou — their name for the Great Spirit.

William's family, the people of the crane clan, claim the honor of being the first Ojibways to pitch their wigwams and light their fires on Shaug-ah-waum-ik-ong, a peninsula directly opposite La Pointe Island. William remembered hearing this legend told around a council fire at La Pointe when he was a young man, and he later wrote it down in his book in these words:

The Great Spirit once made a bird, and he sent it from the skies to make its abode on earth. The bird came, and when it reached half way down, among the clouds, it sent forth a loud and far sounding cry, which was heard by all who resided on the earth....When the bird reached within sight of the earth, it circled slowly above the Great Fresh Water Lakes, and again it uttered its echoing cry. Nearer and nearer it circled, looking for a resting place, till it lit on a hill overlooking Boweting (Sault Sainte Marie); here it chose its first resting place, pleased with the numerous white fish that glanced and swam in the clear waters and sparkling foam of the rapids....

Once again it took its flight, and the bird flew slowly over the waters of Lake Superior. Pleased with the sand point of Shaug-ah-waum-ik-ong, it circled over it, and viewed the numerous fish as they swam about in the clear depths of the Great Lake. It lit on Shaug-ah-waum-ik-ong, and from thence again it uttered its solitary cry. A voice came from the calm bosom of the lake, in answer; the bird, pleased with the musical sound of the voice, again sent forth its cry, and the answering bird made its appearance in the wampum-breasted Loon. The bird spoke to it in a gentle tone, "Is it thou that gives answer to my cry?" The Loon answered, "It is I." The bird then said to him, "Thy voice is music — it is melody — it sounds sweet in my ear, from henceforth I appoint thee to answer my voice in Council."

Thus the Loon became the first in council, but he who made him chief was the Bus-in-aus-e (Echo Maker), or Crane. These are the words of my ancestors, who, from generation to generation, have repeated them into the ears of their children.

In 1825 there were a few posts of white traders and mission stations in the area, but La Pointe Island had no active government. The little government that did exist was in the hands of the fur traders and the Ojibways. The region was peaceful, for most people obeyed the laws.

Another name for the Ojibway Indians is the Chippewas. They were excellent hunters and they knew how to adjust themselves to their sometimes harsh environment. The winters around Lake Superior were long and often extremely cold. When it was necessary, the Ojibways also knew how to be brave and fierce warriors. In the past they had forced the Sioux Indians from the Lake Superior country and kept the Iroquois to the south of Lake Ontario.

The site of the fur trading post on La Pointe Island had been well chosen. It stood with other buildings on a rise of ground about two hundred yards from the lake.

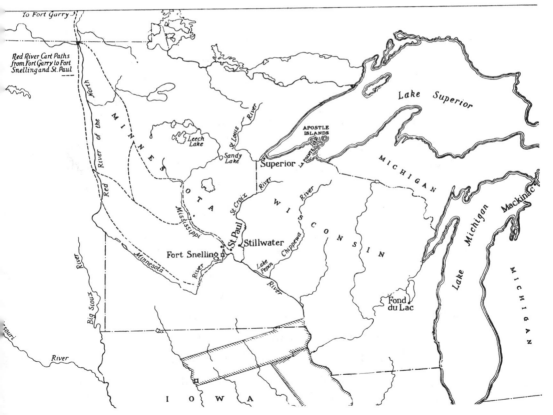

Wisconsin and Minnesota Territories, 1832-1858.

Behind the buildings were plowed fields where oats, peas, beans, and potatoes were grown. The cows and horses had all the grass they wanted to eat. Sugar could be made from the maple trees, and *mah-no-min,* or wild rice, was plentiful. The forests were full of game to be hunted. It was truly, at that time, a good place in which to live.

William's father was Lyman Marquis Warren. He was a descendant of Richard Warren, one of the pilgrims who landed at Plymouth Rock in 1620. Many of the persons who have the name of Warren in the United States are descendants of Richard. These include General Joseph Warren who fell at Bunker Hill, Abraham Warren who fought bravely in the Revolutionary War, and Abraham's son, Stephen, who was also a soldier during the American Revolution. Lyman Warren, another son of Abraham, married Mercy Whipple of Berkshire, Massachusetts. Their son was Lyman Marquis Warren.

Lyman Marquis, William's father, came to the Lake Superior region in 1818. His brother Truman came with him and they both went to work in the fur trade. The two brothers took jobs with Michel Cadotte, who had been a trader among the Ojibways at La Pointe for a long time, Monsieur Cadotte was also the father of two beautiful daughters, Mary and Charlotte, a fact that the Warren brothers were quick to notice. In 1821 Lyman married Mary and Truman chose Charlotte as his wife. Monsieur Cadotte sold out all his trading business to them and he himself retired. There was great sadness four years later, however, when Truman died on board a ship on Lake Superior. He caught a bad cold that turned into pneumonia, which was not unusual during those cold winters in the north country. After his brother's death, Lyman entered into a partnership with the American Fur Company and continued to make La Pointe his headquarters as a trader.

William's relatives on his mother's side were also interesting people. Mary Cadotte came from a family of Ojibway and French descent. For a long time they were known as the aristocrats of the Great Lakes area. They were attractive, energetic people, who were praised for their honesty and business ability.

William Warren's great-grandparents were John Baptiste Cadotte and his Ojibway wife, the daughter of the chief of the crane clan. Monsieur Cadotte was a French trader who had much influence over the Lake Superior Ojibways. It was he who persuaded them not to join with the great chief, Pontiac, in his fight against the English before and at the time of the Revolutionary War. Madame Cadotte, his Ojibway wife, was a very active woman who had great force of character. She is noted to this day for the influence she held over her relatives, who were the most important chiefs and elders of the tribe. Many times she made long journeys to distant villages of her people, traveling alone except for the Canadian trappers who paddled her canoes.

Madame Cadotte was a woman who desired and knew the value of peace in her land. One interesting story told about her is how she saved the life of the British trader, Alexander Henry. Henry was staying at the fort at Mackinaw when a band of Indians arrived, threatening to kill him because he was English. These Indians had fought at the seige of Detroit and had good reason not to like the English. Frightened, Henry decided to go to Sault Sainte Marie where he knew the Indians were peaceful. He also hoped that Monsieur Cadotte would help him.

He left Mackinaw during the night with his Ojibway friend Wa-wa-tam, stopping at an island on the way to Sault Sainte Marie for rest. Then the wife of Wa-wa-tam became very ill and they had to remain there for several days. The delay added to their fears because unfriendly Indians were expected to pass by any day on their way to join other Indian tribes who were fighting against the British. Henry felt a great relief when he at last saw a canoe approaching which he knew must be paddled by Canadians. He could tell they were not Indians by the way they used their canoe paddles. The canoe was actually one that was taking Madame Cadotte to Sault Sainte Marie. When they met she agreed to take him with her. So that he would not look like an Englishman, she had him dress like a Canadian. He wore a blanket coat over his shirt and tied a handkerchief around his head. In the north country hats were worn very little.

On the second day of their voyage, they saw several canoes behind them. As they approached, Henry saw that they were the very Indians from whom he was trying to escape. They came up and surrounded the Cadotte canoe. They talked in general terms at first and asked questions about the news. But before long they began to ask special questions of Henry. He pretended not to understand anything they said. Madame Cadotte spoke to the Indians and gave them the impression that Henry was a Canadian whom she had brought on his first voyage from Montreal. The Indians were satisfied and left.

Why did Madame Cadotte want to give the impression to her red brothers that Henry was a Canadian? Because both she and her husband felt it was a mistake for the Ojibways to continue to fight the British. Many of the Ojibways had fought with the French against the English at Quebec and at other northern forts. The Ojibways felt more loyalty for the French, who were the first white men to come and live their way of life. The French adapted very easily to Indian culture and a great friendship existed between them. But when the French were defeated by the English, the Cadottes had to accept the fact that France's power in the New World was at an end. They knew it would be foolish for the Ojibways to keep up the battle. It would only mean many deaths and cause great sorrow among their people. For this reason Monsieur Cadotte used his influence with the Lake Superior Ojibways to persuade them to stay out of the fight with the English. And this was why Madame Cadotte protected Alexander Henry, an Englishman, from the anger of her own people.

William Warren's grandfather, Michel Cadotte, son of John Baptiste and Madame Cadotte, also married an Indian girl. Beautiful La Pointe Island was named Madeline after this girl, William's grandmother, who was given the island as her wedding present. Weddings among the Ojibways were times of gay celebration and great feasting. Indians from all around the community gathered to take part in the fun and excitement. Some traveled far distances and stayed many days. The marriage of Michel Cadotte to the lovely Ojibway maiden was cause for a very special affair. The Indians were most pleased that the daughter of their powerful and respected chief, White Crane, was to marry the son of the French trader whom they all loved and admired. The celebration of this important marriage lasted for several days. Good things to eat were served for all. There was corn and deer meat and a variety of fruits and other good things that the Indian women prepared. There was much singing and dancing and beating of the drum.

The high point of the ceremony came when White Crane, who was then head chief of the La Pointe Island Ojibways, presented his daughter with the island as a wedding gift. White Crane made a speech with the presentation in which he gave his blessing to the bride and groom and wished them long years of happiness and good living. Then he said, "I give this island to my daughter, for it is mine to give, and it shall be called Madeline."

With such a prize as their very own the bride and groom made the town of La Pointe, on Madeline Island, their home. They opened a trading post there and started a small settlement in this beautiful wilderness setting. The island and fur trading post at La Pointe was a home for many generations of the Cadotte and Warren families. It was here that William's father Lyman Warren came to work in Michel Cadotte's fur trade business, married Mary Cadotte, and eventually took over the La Pointe post. Here at La Pointe is where William Warren grew up.

CHAPTER II

Fur Trading
in Ojibway Land

The business of trading furs played an important part in the development of the land where William Warren was raised. William's mother's father and her grandfather were pioneer fur traders in the Lake Superior area. His own father and uncle made their living as fur traders. The man who was to become his father-in-law, William Aitkin, was one of the more famous fur traders of his time.

Many years before William was born, a company of French traders came up the west coast of Lake Superior and built the first trading post. In those days it was called a "fort," from the French word meaning "strong." At that time there were great quantities of beaver along all the streams that emptied into Lake Superior. The traders found that the Ojibways who lived in the area were very peaceful and friendly. The French also liked the dignified, quiet character of the Ojibways.

The fur trade was very important to the development of our country. The trading of furs was the first business carried on in North America. French explorers were the first to be fur traders. The French noticed that many Indians wore clothes that they had made of fur or animal skins. The furs the Indians wore came from the mink, beaver, deer, fox, bear, and other wild animals that they hunted. The Frenchmen offered the Indians warm blankets, knives, kettles, guns, and colored jewelry for the furs. The Indians were happy to trade. They made good use of the kettles and blankets. They saw immediately that steel knives were better for cutting than stone. They also wanted the guns that were better than their bows and arrows for hunting or protection from their enemies.

The people in Europe wanted furs to keep them warm. Beaver hats and coats were especially popular. When the explorers collected enough furs, they would sail back to France and sell them. The fur trade on our continent started in this simple manner. Of course, as time passed more and more people began to work as fur traders. One well-known trader was Henry H. Sibley, who later

American Fur Company post at Fond du Lac, 1826.
(From McKenney, Sketches of a Tour to the Lakes.*)*

became Minnesota's first governor. As the industry grew, trading companies were formed. Some of the biggest companies, whose names you may have heard before, were Hudson's Bay Company, run by the English; Northwest Company, owned by the French; and the American Fur Company, owned by John Jacob Astor. It was the American Fur Company with whom William's father made a contract. These companies competed against each other until 1816. In that year Congress passed an act prohibiting foreigners from entering the fur trade in the United States, and from then on Mr. Astor had the trade all to himself.

Trading posts such as the one where William lived as a boy were important, but the men who owned these big companies also needed men to take trading goods westward into Indian country in the spring of each year and come back each fall with the furs they had gathered. Without these men, who became known as "voyageurs," the companies would not have been able to stay in business. *Voyageur* is a French word that means "traveler." The voyageur, who was well known to the Ojibways, was in a class by himself. He wore a special kind of clothes and he had his own customs and way of life. The voyageurs got along well with the Indians. Many of them, after a time, gave up their traveling life, married Indian girls, settled in Indian villages, and were good husbands and good fathers to their children.

The voyageur was very colorful in his dress. He is usually pictured in a bright long-sleeved shirt and trousers that have a little sash tied below each knee. The sash had a useful purpose. It kept his trousers from binding his knees as he sat in the canoe. Sometimes he tied a very long bright sash around his waist too. For his feet he traded with the Indians for brightly decorated deerskin moccasins. In winter he made himself a hooded coat from one of his blankets. Voyageurs loved red. On their heads they often wore a red stocking cap with a feather stuck in it.

Voyageurs were small men physically. It was really necessary for them not to be big because there was very little room in a canoe for a man who had long legs. But they were strong; they had to be to paddle a canoe all day. Voyageurs are probably best remembered for their gaiety. Their laughter and songs could be heard floating across the wilderness lakes. Some say they sang and danced so much because the journeys they took were very dangerous and they put on a bold front of songs and laughter to keep their spirits up and not think about the danger.

The canoes used by these first fur traders were made of birch bark just as the Indian canoes were. But because of their love of bright colors the voyageurs often painted their canoes. They also painted their cedarwood paddles red.

A pipe for smoking was something every voyageur owned. About once every hour he would stop and rest and smoke his pipe. It was by the number of "pipes" that they measured the streams and lakes. They measured their portages over land by how many "poses." "Pose" also comes from a French word and means "to put something down." If the portage distance were short, the voyageur would carry his packs all the way before he returned for another. On a long portage the men broke the distance by a series of poses. Each man would carry his load to a resting place along the way and then put it down. The whole cargo, and even the canoe, would be brought to this place before anyone went any farther. About one-third of a mile was usually the distance between poses. Some portages were so long that they were divided into as many as 122 poses.

There were two kinds of voyageurs. The "pork-eaters" were the ones who returned to their home base for the winter. The "winterers" were those who stayed and made trips to other posts or to Indian villages during the winter. The "winterers" used snowshoes and a dog sled to carry their cargo. The husky dogs understood only French. When a voyageur wanted his team to "go" he yelled out the French word *marche*. Even today whenever dog sleds are used in America you will hear the driver using this word — only pronouncing it "mush."

The voyageur lived a life full of adventure, but it was a hard-working life, too, with many hardships. Even so he is best remembered for his light heart, good humor, and gay and lively songs. Today in northern Minnesota there is a canoe camp for boys and girls called "Voyageur's Landing," where the campers set out in canoes every summer to follow some of the routes of the voyageurs. As they paddle over the lakes and carry their packs over the portages between them, they sing some of the voyageurs' old songs and try to remember that voyageurs never complain even when the going gets mighty rough.

The fur trading industry in Minnesota began to fail

when it became fashionable to make hats out of materials other than fur. Silk, for example, was one of the new popular items. The whole picture of fur trading in America began to change when clothes started to be made by machine. After that, fur, which had been a part of nearly everyone's wardrobe, became more of a luxury and the demand for furs dropped. As a result, the big companies, who were in the fur trade strictly to make money, went out of business. By the time William Warren went away to school in 1836, the peak of the fur trade had passed.

As one voyageur lights his pipe,
others bring furs into their canoe.

CHAPTER III

Childhood
in the North Country

The first years of William Warren's life were spent in a large and comfortable house that was one of the trading post buildings on Madeline Island. This was the island owned by his grandmother and grandfather, who were the first to build a house and trading post there. The houses and other buildings of both families resembled a small village. The Indians called Madeline, or La Pointe Island, Mon-ing-wum-a-kaun-ing, which means "the place of the golden-breasted woodpecker." Although there were many birds and much wildlife on the island, the Indians thought the woodpecker was the most out-standing.

Until he was seven years old William spoke only Ojibway. This was the language his family spoke. His father knew how to speak English but he rarely did so; he was content to make his home among his wife's people. William was a charming child and soon became a favorite with the fur traders and missionaries. Life was pleasant for him, and he spent many hours playing with his brother and sisters and the other Indian children on the island.

Indian children, like all other children, love to play games. William and his friends had many games that they would play by the hour. Through these games they exercised their fingers and senses, developing skills that would be necessary later as they began to hunt and fish. One clever game was played with pins. The boys would beg the straight pins from their mother and then lie down on the grass to play. The game went like this. First, a piece of grass would be smoothed down and one of the children would throw a pin on it. Another would then give his pin a flip with his finger, trying to make his pin cross the first pin. If he succeeded he won the first pin. Skilled fingers and wrists were required for this and the children's aim was as sure with the pins as with the bow and arrow.

Some days they would walk along the shores of the lake and collect the oval stones that were found on the banks. They would save them to use on the ice in the winter. Surefooted and swift, they would run over the ice in the winter and drive the stones against each other with whips and sticks. The stone that upset the other was the winner. These boys would certainly have made good hockey players if skates had been available then.

Pagessan was a popular game too. It was often played by the older Indians as well. French traders called it "the game of the bowl." It was played with a wooden bowl and a number of small figures which represented such things as a fish, hand, door, man, canoe, half-moon, and so forth. These figures were carved very neatly out of bones, wood, or plum stones. Each figure had a foot on which it could stand upright. They were all thrown into the wooden bowl. Then the players would make a hole in the ground and push the bowl into the hole while giving the bowl a slight shake. The more figures that would be left standing upright on the smooth bottom of the bowl through this shake, the higher the score for the player. Each figure would have its own value. There were also other figures carved into small round shapes that did not have a foot on the bottom of them. These were red on one side and plain on the other and would be counted as plus or minus depending on which side ended up. To win this game, a great deal depended on the skill with which the bowl was shaken. As William grew older he and his friends would spend hours playing this game. They took pagessan very seriously and would often screech and yell with excitement while playing it.

William and the other boys were also very clever at making things with their hands. One of the things his sisters begged for was tops. He would make several for them every year out of acorns and nuts.

La Pointe, Madeline Island, in 1898.
Photo by S. W. Bailey, Ashland, Wisconsin.

Listening to the elders tell stories was a favorite pastime for the youngsters, too. This proved to be a good education for William, because his memory was sharp and clear and he remembered in detail many of the things he heard from the old men. When he was older he would put many of these stories into writing for all people to read.

Often the leading character in the old stories was the Ojibway hero, Manabosho. The Ojibways believed that the wise Gitche Manitou, or Great Spirit, had sent them Manabosho to be their teacher.

Manabosho was the son of Wenonah and the grandson of Nokomis, a wise old woman who was a daughter of the Moon. Actually Manabosho was a twin, but his brother died at birth and his mother departed with her dead son to the land of the spirits. Nokomis felt great sorrow at the loss of her daughter and one of her grandsons, but she wrapped the living child in soft grass and called him Manabosho. Because he was the son of the West Wind and the great-grandson of the Moon, Manabosho was more than human and could change himself into many marvelous things. Sometimes he would be a bear or a tree, or even a snake or a rabbit, but his favorite shape was that of a strong young Indian brave. One day, dressed as a handsome brave, he decided to travel up a nearby river all the way to its source. As he paddled his canoe along the route he came upon a solid wall of rock under which the river flowed. He raised the great club he was carrying and struck the rock a very hard blow. The rock split into two huge cliffs and the river rushed between them, soaking him with spray. With disgust he flung off his buckskin robe because it was useless now that it was wet. The robe hardened against the rock as it dried until it became like stone. In Ojibway country there is a rock where, if you look closely, you can still see the shape of the robe. The people call the rock "Manabosho's blanket."

After a while Manabosho wandered up to the mighty falls far above him. While there he seemed to hear spirit voices in the loud sound of the water, telling him that his time on earth was growing short. At dusk a flying squirrel glided down and rested upon his shoulder as if to comfort him.

Little by little the thought came to Manabosho that there should be some way to record all the things he saw. He kept the thought in his mind, and one day as he was paddling his great canoe along the shore of Gitche Gume, he noticed again the smooth face of the rocks that rose from the water. He was struck by an idea. Here would be just the place to put drawings of the things of the earth!

Excited, he paddled his canoe to the shore and began looking around for some material that would be right for his work. He looked for some time before he noticed there were streaks of red among the rocks. (Today, we call these "red streaks" iron oxide.) With a sharp stone he scraped out some of the red pigment, crushed it between two rocks, and turned it into powder. After this he made a bowl out of birch bark and placed the powder in it to carry back to the water's edge. He started work eagerly, but when he tried to paint on the rocks with the powder, it blew away in the wind.

Manabosho was discouraged but he did not give up. He knew he must find something that would make the powder stick to the smooth rock face. Then he noticed a gull's nest on the cliff. He reached up and removed some of the eggs from the nest while the gulls screamed and beat their wings about him. Manabosho chased off the birds and then broke open the eggs and mixed them with the red powder to make a sticky paste. He tried some of this mixture on the rocks and was very happy to find it did not blow away.

Now that he knew how to do it, Manabosho made a great deal of the paint and put it into his canoe. He paddled close to the steep cliff and then stood up carefully in the canoe. With his fingers he began to make drawings on the face of the rock. First he drew a row of spruce trees to represent the forest. Then he drew a young deer and a cow moose with her calf. He paused a moment and drew a big old bear that he had seen in the forest that morning. Manabosho was so pleased with himself and his new skill that he spent many days painting his designs and pictures on the rocks.

One sunny afternoon he was working on a cliff face high above the lake. An Ojibway chief came paddling along the shore. This chief was wise and he was always ready to teach his people new things. He had already tried to make picture writings of his own but had not been successful, so he was filled with excitement as he looked up at the drawings that Manabosho was making. He called to Manabosho, but the big man pretended not to hear and went on with his work. Finally the chief looked about for some way of getting closer to the drawings to study them.

The sheer face of the rock stretched high above him and he noted that Manabosho was working at the highest place. The chief took his tomahawk and began to cut steps in the face of the cliff. He worked away for many hours, chopping a stairway to the place where Manabosho was working. Finally, after much hard work he arrived at a step where he could see the drawings up close. When Manabosho saw him there, he gave him a nudge and the chief lost his footing and fell headlong back down into the water. The poor chief was most unhappy. He feared that Manabosho would finish his work before he could climb back again. So as soon as he pulled himself out of the water he began the long climb once more.

Manabosho watched the chief with interest. He knew that if he was to pass on his newfound knowledge to the people he would have to teach the secret to someone. The person chosen would have to be worthy of the knowledge. Perhaps this brave chief who refused to give up was just the man. Manabosho bent down and spoke to the chief.

"What is it you are looking for? Why did you cut these steps in the rock?"

"O Mighty One," answered the chief, "teach me the magic of this great sign language that I may tell my people. I can see it is a great and wise thing."

Manabosho was pleased with the answer that was given him. He waited for the chief to reach him before he began work again. As he painted he told the secret meanings of the picture writing to the chief.

The day was very warm, for it was in the middle of the summer. Often Manabosho would stop and wipe the sweat from his face with his fingers. He was thirsty and bent down to get a drink, but was startled to see a terrible face looking up at him from the lake. The face had black hair and eyes like his, but the rest of the face was striped with red. He reached for his tomahawk and aimed blow after blow at the face in the water. For a moment it would be gone, but as soon as the water settled it would be there again.

To his amazement, Manabosho noticed that the chief was watching him and shaking with laughter. It was then he realized that he had been fighting his own reflection in the water, which had looked terrible because his face was streaked with paint from his fingers. Remembering this experience, Manabosho later taught the people how to paint their faces to frighten their enemies in battle.

The wise chief learned from Manabosho where to get the red pigment for color and how to mix it into a paste that would cling to the rocks. The chief in turn taught the secret to his people. It was in this way that the Ojibways learned to make pictures of the things they knew in the world of man. They also made pictures of what they imagined life was like in the land of the spirits.

Many times when William was trying to learn how to write English, he thought he knew how the old chief must have felt when Manabosho explained the secret meanings of the picture writing to him. But like the chief, William did not give up, and he learned his lessons well.

CHAPTER IV

School Years
in New York

When he was seven, William began attending the Indian School at La Pointe that was run by Reverend William T. Boutwell. The next year he went to the mission school at Mackinaw. He studied at this school until he was eleven years old. Then in 1836 his grandfather, Lyman Warren, who was then living in New York, visited them at their family home. He had not seen his grandchildren before and took a great liking to them. When he returned to the East he took William and his brother Truman with him so that they could go to school in New York. It must have been both a glad and a sad time for the family. The parents of course wanted the best possible education for their children, but they knew how much they would miss them and how lonesome the four sisters would be for their two brothers.

For two years William went to school in Clarkson, New York, and from 1838 to 1841 he attended the Oneida Institute at Whitesborough near Utica, New York. Here he acquired a good knowledge of English. Before he went East for school, of course, he did not speak English; Ojibway was the language spoken at home and by practically all the people he knew. Now William learned to write well in English, and he found that he loved to read. He spent hours reading. All books were interesting to him.

William was a popular boy in school. He was full of life, cheerful, and his classmates found him great fun to be with. He was an even-tempered person who never really got upset about things. Although he was a bit shy, the training he received at school helped him to be more confident.

While William and his brother Truman were still going to school at the Clarkson Academy, his mother with her four girls, Charlotte, Julia, Mary, and Sophia, decided to make a trip East to visit Grandfather Warren and the two boys. You can imagine the excitement at La Pointe when mother and girls decided to make this big trip. They planned a long time, for there was much to do to get ready. There were new clothes to make and all kinds of things to talk about. This was the first long trip the girls or their mother had ever made away from home and everyone at the settlement pitched in to help them. There was lots of fuss and bustle and laughter and tears when the time came for them to leave.

They traveled in the summer when the weather was good and the trip would be easier and more comfortable, but it still took them a long time to go from La Pointe to New York. They had to travel most of the time by stagecoach, because railroad connections were poor and there were no airplanes.

This was an exciting time for William, too. He had done well in school in the East, but there were many times when he was lonesome for his family and the life he had known at La Pointe. It helped to have his brother with him, but he was pleased and happy to hear his mother and sisters were coming to visit. Now they'd have all the news of home!

There was great joy when his mother and sisters finally reached Grandfather's house. They visited for many weeks with Grandfather Warren. The older man took great pleasure in showing the family around the big city. Before Mrs. Warren went home, a big decision was made. Charlotte and Julia, the two older girls, were to stay at Grandfather's so they could go to school too. Late in the summer, Mrs. Warren took Mary and Sophia and began the long journey back to La Pointe.

The next few years passed by quickly; there were now four Warren children to keep one another company while they were away from home. They were still lonesome at times, but Grandfather was good and kind and four of them together seemed more like a family.

CHAPTER V

The Return
to Ojibway Land

William was sixteen when he returned from New York. From this time on he took a man's part in all affairs. Sixteen may seem young, but Indian males were often considered men at that age.

Before he left La Pointe he had spoken only Ojibway. When he was going to school in New York only English was used. On his return he found that he had forgotten some of the Ojibway language. But he soon became familiar with it again and learned to use it remarkably well. He was a welcome guest around the lodge-fire circles, and he developed a great fondness for Ojibway legends and traditions. Later on, when William was writing his book, he would tell of the love he had for these stories and legends of his Indian grandfathers. One of his favorites was the story of how Manabosho brought fire to his people.

In the early times of the world the Ojibway people had no fire to keep them warm or to cook their food. They were also afraid of fire because they had seen what it could do to the forest when lightning struck.

Fire was kept in the underworld. Once a coyote went

to the underworld and brought back some fire, but the people were afraid of it and would not use it. They sought out an old warrior-magician to guard it and protect them from it. Sometimes a few of the more adventurous braves would try to steal the fire from the old man, but they never succeeded. With the help of his two daughters he always guarded it well.

Manabosho at this time was young and strong and the lack of fire meant little to him, but his grandmother, Nokomis, was old and the cold seemed to go right through her. In the winter she would sit huddled in her fur robe and complain that she was freezing. One day Manabosho came into the wigwam and found her shivering. He tried to cheer her up.

"Come, Nokomis," he said, "let's follow the hunting trail in the forest. We will move swiftly and the blood will soon be warm in your veins."

Nokomis looked the other way and settled down further into her fur robe. "That's fine for you," she said, "but I am old and must move slowly. Hunting trails are no longer for me. I am cold and the wind bites me to the middle of my bones."

Manabosho felt very sorry for his grandmother and brought her a piece of meat. He hoped the food would make her feel better. But the raw deer meat was frozen solid. Old Nokomis's teeth were not very strong any more and she could not eat the meat. As Manabosho watched her he made a promise that before another winter came he would steal some fire for his grandmother so she would not have to be cold anymore.

The next fall, in the month of the wild rice, which is

September, he started for the place where the old warrior-magician was guarding the fire. When he got close to the old man's home he hid his canoe in the trees. Then he turned himself into a white rabbit and jumped into the water so that he would look wet and pitiful. He hoped this would make the two daughters feel sorry for him.

His plan worked. One of the girls saw him and picked him up and carried him inside. She set him down near the burning fire so he would dry off and warm himself. Then she went back to her work.

Manabosho hopped a little closer to the fire, waiting for a chance to steal some. His movements woke the old magician who had been sleeping in a corner.

"What was that noise?" the old man asked.

Then he saw the rabbit and became suspicious. He got up to have a better look at him, but the small white rabbit seemed so innocent that the old man went back to his corner and was soon asleep again.

When Manabosho heard the old man snoring he changed himself from a rabbit into an Indian brave, grabbed the fire, and ran from the lodge with it. Swiftly he ran toward his hidden canoe.

The old magician woke up and knew right away exactly what had happened. He shouted to the girls to chase Manabosho and bring back the sacred fire. Manabosho ran as fast as he could down the trail, very sure that he could outrun two girls. But when he looked over his shoulder he was surprised to see that they were gaining on him. He doubled his speed, but the girls, by means of magic, ran faster still.

"Give us back our fire," they yelled. "Give us back our fire!"

By then Manabosho had reached his canoe. He glanced back and saw a large meadow of dried grass. "Here is your fire," he yelled, and with that he plunged the burning stick into the grass. The grass immediately caught on fire and the wind carried the flames and smoke back toward the girls so that they could not follow him.

As Manabosho looked back to watch the fire burn in the meadow, he noticed how the colors of the fire were reflected in the broad-leafed trees. The leaves shone in brilliant shades of red and gold and bronze. He thought it was so beautiful that he decided to make leaves look that way every year in the fall.

When the fire had spread enough so that the two girls could not return to catch him, he put the burning stick in one end of his canoe and paddled swiftly back to his people. When he reached home he gave his gift of fire to Nokomis and she was very thankful for the heat it gave her.

When the people saw that fire could do many good things for them, they soon lost their fear of fire and put it to many uses. They were grateful to Manabosho and would tell over and over again, in days to come, how he had brought them fire.

In return for the old men telling him their favorite stories, William would translate into their language various stories he thought they would like — stories from the Bible, tales from the Arabian Nights, and many

others. He loved books and was always able to remember
a good tale from the books he had read. The Indians
were very fond of William, not just because he was a
relative, but because he was kind and considerate of
them. He showed a real interest in their welfare and
was always anxious to help them in any way he could.
This was the Ojibway way of life — to care deeply for
one another and to share one's possessions freely with
others. This held true not only among relatives but
between all members of the tribe. And this sharing was
not looked upon as "giving gifts" or "helping" or
"lending." To share and help one another was part of
each Ojibway's right as a member of the tribe. William
was raised with this attitude and it became a characteristic
part of his nature.

It is difficult for many people to understand this spirit
of sharing, because it is a "code," a way of life, that is
different from most cultures. The Indian system places
no value on the owning of more and more material
things. There is perhaps nothing in the Indian heritage
that has been so greatly misunderstood by others as their
value system. Through William's efforts, the "communi-
cation gap" between Indians and non-Indians was made
smaller. He had an excellent relationship with non-Indians
and they had great admiration and respect for him.
Through William's life and the words he was to write,
people of different ways and color were able to understand a little better the Indian people he represented.

William was only seventeen when Reverend Alfred
Brunson came to La Pointe as a government representative. Reverend Brunson did not speak Ojibway and

needed someone who understood and spoke Ojibway well to act as an interpreter for him. He chose William as his aide. He found William to be so skillful that he told other people if they ever needed an interpreter they should choose William. Many did, and in the next few years William often worked as an interpreter, becoming quite skilled at it. One of the government officials for whom William was an interpreter, Henry M. Rice, said that William was one of the most "eloquent and fluent" speakers he ever heard, with a remarkable, and even musical, command of both languages.

In the summer of 1842, William married Matilda Aitkin. She was the daughter of William A. Aitkin, a well-known fur trader. Matilda was part Ojibway and part Scottish. Her mother was from a well-known Ojibway family. Her father was a Scotsman in charge of the Fond du Lac department of the American Fur Company. It was Mr. Aitkin who convinced the missionary, Frederick Ayer, to open a school at Sandy Lake, Minnesota. The school was started in 1833 for the children of the fur traders, boatmen, and guides. Many years later Mr. Aitkin had a Minnesota county and also a Minnesota town named after him.

William continued to work as an interpreter after he was married. In this kind of work he often had to go with his employer on long and difficult trips. In 1844-1845, traveling with the Indian agent I. P. Hays, he began developing lung trouble from his frequent exposure to the severe winter cold. This lung trouble was to be the cause of much suffering in the years ahead, and William was never able to recover from it completely.

In the first year of his marriage William happened to see a very strange and interesting family register. It can probably be compared to that part of some Christian Bibles where family records are kept. The old chief who owned the register kept it carefully buried in the ground and seldom brought it out. It had been entrusted to his care by someone from the generation before him, and he, in turn, would pass it on for safekeeping to someone in the next generation.

The register was a plate of copper with eight deep grooves in it. These grooves stood for the number of his ancestors who had died since his family had first pitched its lodges at Shaug-ah-waum-ik-ong and nearby Madeline Island. Opposite one of the grooves was the figure of a man with a hat on his head. This mark showed when the white man had first made his appearance among them — during the third generation of this family.

William's uncle, Tug-waug-aum-ay, was about sixty years old when he showed the Warrens this plate of copper. In 1844, two years later, he died. His death added the ninth groove on the plate. Thus, in 1844 there had been nine generations of Ojibways living on Madeline Island, and six generations since the white man had first come into that region.

All the Indians in this family knew of the plate of copper and what it meant. The parents told their children about it and the children passed the story on to their children. In this way alone, by word of mouth, the Ojibways kept their history alive for future generations. They never had a written language. It was left to William, who had learned English, to put their history down in written form.

CHAPTER VI

From Crow Wing
to Two Rivers

In 1845 William and his brother Truman moved to Crow Wing, Minnesota, with their families. Crow Wing was a settlement that was born of the fur trade, and the years between 1841 and 1848 were a time of expansion. The Warren families were part of this growth. Crow Wing was given added importance in 1845 when it became a part of the Red River Trail, as a result of trouble with Sioux Indian uprisings. The ox carts of settlers were searching for a new route to the West that would bypass Sioux land, and they crossed the settlement of Crow Wing. At this time a Saint Paul stagecoach line ended at Crow Wing also, adding to its prosperity.

Lumber business came next and then the town really boomed. Miss Elizabeth Ayer arrived in 1846 to start the first school there. This adventurous young woman was paid the sum of thirty-six dollars a month and had twelve pupils in her classroom.

Crow Wing's prosperous years ended abruptly when the railroad company decided to bypass Crow Wing and go on to Brainerd. It took only thirty years for this village to begin and end. The Warren brothers and their families lived there for two years during the prosperous times. William had a job as a farmer and interpreter for Major J. E. Fletcher, who was the government agent in charge of the Mississippi Ojibways.

Also living near Crow Wing at this time was a young Indian called Hole-in-the-Day, an Ojibway chief whose father, Hole-in-the-Day the Elder, had also been a chief. Hole-in-the-Day lived in a large and comfortable frame house on a nice farm covering one square mile of land. He had a large stock of horses and cattle.

William had known this young man and also his father since he had been a small boy. In fact everyone who had been born and raised in this area knew of them. The father and son were alike in many ways. Hole-in-the-Day the Elder had not become a chief by hereditary right; that is, it was not passed down to him from his father or a brother. The Ojibway Indians did recognize hereditary chieftainship, but this was not the only way men could become chiefs. Hole-in-the-Day the Elder, for example, became a chief in 1825 at the dying request of the old Ojibway chief Curly Head, who had no children of his own to succeed him.

Hole-in-the-Day the Elder was a powerful speaker. Sometimes during councils he would have his listeners so wrapped up in what he was saying that in the most exciting parts they would actually leap from their seats. In great excitement they would fill the air with their yells.

Hole-in-the-Day the Elder had many daring adventures on the warpath and at an early age was wearing a feather in his hair, signifying that he had killed one of the Ojib-ways' enemies. Young Hole-in-the-Day also earned his feather at an early age. The father and son became known as brave warriors, much feared by their enemies the Sioux.

When Hole-in-the-Day the Elder was thrown from a wagon and killed in 1847, Hole-in-the-Day took over his father's position as chief. His first appearance as chief came in July, 1847, during a council held between government commissioners and Ojibways at Fond du Lac, Wisconsin. The government wished to obtain from the Ojibway Indians the land called the Upper Country of the Mississippi that lies between the Wattap and Crow Wing rivers. Through his influence the Indians accepted the treaty with the government. From this time on, Hole-in-the-Day was influential in signing a number of treaties between the Ojibways and the government.

Hole-in-the-Day was loyal to the Union during the Civil War. At one time he wanted to raise a battalion of Ojibways and send them forth upon the warpath to help fight the battles of the Union. He was disappointed when the government did not accept his offer.

In the early 1860s his large frame house burned to the ground. The government gave him five thousand dollars as payment for his loss. He then built himself a comfortable log house and used the rest of the money for the purchase of livestock. He turned his attention to agriculture and raised large crops on his farm. He also had at least a dozen head of good horses.

One day in 1868 he had one of his famed horses hitched to a handsome, light, one-horse buggy and was on his way home from Crow Wing with another Ojibway Indian named Ojibbewa. It was on this day he was assassinated by a band of nine Pillager Indians who were waiting to

The Story of William Warren 38

ambush him. Just as the buggy was going past the thick woods in which the Pillagers were hiding, they rushed out and surrounded the buggy. After robbing his body, they took a back route to his house and robbed it, too. Then they departed for Leech Lake where their band was located. Ojibbewa was not killed but he was taken prisoner. Later he was released and lived to tell the story of the murder.

Many reasons were given for the murder but no one knows for sure what the correct one was. Some said it was jealousy. Others said the Pillagers felt they had been cheated in some of the treaties that Hole-in-the-Day had signed with the government. Hole-in-the-Day was buried in the cemetery at Crow Wing, only forty years old at the time of his death.

Soon after William Warren moved to Crow Wing, he was hired by the government to do an important job. He was to go to Chippewa Falls, Wisconsin, and bring all the male Indians living in that area to Sandy Lake to get their yearly payment from the government. The government also wanted the Indians to look over the country around Sandy Lake to see if they liked it. If it met with their approval they would be moved to that location the next year. William's health was very poor at this time. His sister Julia, who lived at Chippewa Falls, urged him to take her with him so she could take care of him if he became sick. William finally agreed and they started on their journey.

They traveled by canoe up the Chippewa River to Lac Countereille and waited there for two days until they were joined by the Indians who were going to travel with them to Sandy Lake. Finally they arrived and the group started through the woods at *wah-bun,* which means "the break of day." They traveled very slowly because the Indians had to pack their own canoes and some of them spent a great deal of time hunting. There was lots of game in the woods and along the river banks. They killed bear, deer, geese, and ducks. They had brought plenty of wild rice with them so they all had more than enough to eat each day.

After traveling many days they reached Lake Superior and camped near the mouth of the Saint Louis River. There were now several hundred Indians in the group. It was here that William became very sick. His diseased lungs began to bleed and it was necessary for him to remain still and quiet while his sister cared for him. When he was well enough to travel again, he called all the Indians together and told them he had something he wanted to say to them. Then he pointed toward the spot where the city of Duluth now stands and said, "One day there will be a great city there. The lake around it will be full of all kinds of vessels." Then he pointed to where the city of Superior now is and continued, "Over there will be another great city, but not as great as the first city. I will not live to see it, but many of you young men will."

All that William predicted about the future that day came true. Duluth is now an important seaport, the third largest city in Minnesota. Superior is also a thriving city, but true to William's prediction, it is not as large as Duluth. Imagine, though, how surprised the Indians were at that time to hear William say all this. His sister Julia was startled, too. Later on she wrote about the trip she had made with her brother and remembered how she felt when he said what would happen. She wrote, "I don't know what the other Indians thought but I thought my poor brother was losing his mind." It is very probable that many of his red brothers who heard him speak that day felt the same way. The Lake Superior country during the middle 1800s was all wilderness with very few white settlers. It must have seemed to everyone but William that it would always remain that way. Perhaps he had the gift of seeing into the future, and knew how things will be in years to come; if so, perhaps it was a wisdom that came to him because of his closeness to nature and the respect he had for all living things.

After this stop William Warren and his group traveled up the Saint Louis River to Fond du Lac and from there to Sandy Lake. When they arrived, their group was made up of many hundreds of Ojibways who were waiting for their payment. They had to wait two or three weeks longer before the money came. During this time measles broke out, and many also became very ill from eating spoiled pork and flour. A great number of them died. The Wisconsin Indians became very discouraged. They declared they would never go to Sandy Lake for their payment again and they refused to be moved there to live.

Soon after the unfortunate happening at Sandy Lake, William and his wife moved their home to Two Rivers in Morrison County, Minnesota. They now had four children, Alfred, Madeline, William Tyler, and Delia. At Two Rivers they built a home on a beautiful spot, just opposite the mouths of two small rivers that emptied into the Mississippi on the western side, a short distance apart. That is why it was called Two Rivers. Opposite this point in the river there was a lovely little island, and growing all around the house were maple sugar trees from which they would make many pounds of fine sugar in the spring.

Spring was the season when all Ojibway families were busy making sugar; this was the time when the sap began

"Indian Sugar Camp" by Seth Eastman.

to rise in the maple trees, ready to be collected by the women and children. Sugar making usually lasted about six weeks, and it was very hard work. The long sugar-house had to be made ready; it was here that the sap was boiled in large kettles to separate the water from the sugar. Huge piles of wood had to be collected to keep the fires going under the kettles.

The women went from tree to tree, making a gash in the trunks and putting a wood spout in each cut. Underneath each spout they would place a birch bark trough to catch the dripping sap. Children would help by collecting the full troughs, carrying them to the sugar-house, and running back to the trees with them so they could fill up again.

The women boiled the sap down to a heavy syrup, let it cool, then poured it into "boats" of hollowed-out logs, where the sugar syrup was "worked" by hand to just the right consistency. Finally, the finished sugar was stored in birch bark *makuks* to be used throughout the rest of the year.

William and his family loved their new home and were very happy there. Many times friends would come and stay for long visits. They were always welcome, whether they were Indians or non-Indians. William and his family would share their home and whatever they had with their guests.

One of these visitors was his good friend Esk-ke-bug-e-coshe, or Flat Mouth. He was a famous chief of the Pillager band of Ojibways. He enjoyed visiting with William so much that he would travel all the way from Leech Lake for a visit. He was seventy-eight years old at the time but he would still journey that long distance to see William, whom he called his "grandson." For hours the two of them would sit and talk in the Ojibway language. Chief Flat Mouth had a long and eventful life and William planned some day to write a book about the lives of some of the famous Ojibway Indians he had known. Surely Flat Mouth and Hole-in-the-Day and many others would have been in this book, but William died before he had a chance to finish writing it. He also had in mind another book that would have told about Ojibway traditions and legends. He thought of it as an "Indian Bible" through which readers could get a more complete idea of the Ojibway character and beliefs.

You see, these Ojibway stories and legends were used to teach tradition and proper conduct. Not only children, but also their parents, could be taught lessons by the stories. One story that William remembered well was about the "Vision Quest."

The "Vision Quest" is part of the custom of fasting as it was practiced by the early Ojibway people. Children began fasting when they were still very young, even as young as seven years old. The child would know that he was supposed to fast if he woke in the morning and found ashes in his dish. His father expected him to rub these ashes on his face and leave for a lonely place where he would be all by himself, a place where he would have a dream or vision. If he should dream of an animal, that animal then became his guardian spirit. As the child grew older the dreams became more important and would sometimes predict what would happen in the future or explain what had happened in the past.

This is the Vision Quest story that William heard the old men tell around the lodge-fires.

There was once a young boy who had already gone into the woods many times to fast. He thought he had dreamed about everything there was to dream about. But his father insisted that he blacken his face with ashes and fast still more. The young boy obediently went back again into the woods to have another dream. After his vision he would return to the wigwam. His father asked him again to go back and fast longer. The boy obeyed and went on with his fasting. When he returned to the wigwam the father urged him to fast for one more day. The boy fasted for one more day and his father finally told him he could now eat, but when the boy tried to eat he found that he could not. He had fasted too long.

Finding he could not eat food, the boy prepared some paint and painted his face and combed his hair to look like the robin. He wished to be a robin and his wish was granted. He was turned into a robin and flew up on the crossbeams of the wigwam. His father was sad when he saw this and also very sorry he had asked his son to fast for so long. He called and called for the boy to come back, but his son answered, "No, I'm going to be a robin. I will come back in the spring. Then I will feel it in my red breast if the summer will be good or bad, and I will know if there will be war."

This story was told to teach both parents and children not to ask too much of Gitche Manitou, the Great Spirit.

CHAPTER VII

The Council
at Fort Snelling

William Warren played an important part in the council of Sioux and Ojibway Indians which was held at Fort Snelling on June 11, 1850, in an effort to bring peace between them. There had always been trouble between these two tribes, but lately it had been getting worse. At daybreak on April 2, a party of Sioux from Red Wing and Kaposia who were out seeking adventure had attacked an Ojibway sugar camp on the Apple River in Wisconsin. This was about twenty miles from Stillwater, Minnesota. The whole party of fifteen Ojibways was killed. Only one boy escaped and he was taken prisoner. Governor Ramsey of Minnesota, who was in charge of Indian affairs for the Minnesota Territory, decided that some action was called for. He arrested thirteen Sioux warriors and they were sent to jail at Fort Snelling.

About a month later, Hole-in-the-Day came down from Ojibway country with two friends. On the afternoon of May 15, they crossed the Mississippi River and hid their canoe in a ditch. Then, almost in sight of the citizens of Saint Paul, they attacked a small party of Sioux Indians. No one but Hole-in-the-Day would attempt an act such as this. He seemed to be without fear and had no regard for danger. The three Ojibways were chased back across the river by a large number of Sioux, but they managed to escape. Before long the Sioux were seen running through the streets of Saint Paul painted and dressed for war.

When the news reached Governor Ramsey, he decided not to press the charges any further against the men who had been arrested at Apple River. Instead, he called the Sioux and Ojibway chiefs to a council to settle the matter peacefully.

On June 9, a hundred Ojibways led by Hole-in-the-Day arrived at Fort Snelling. The following morning three hundred Sioux came to the treaty ground. The Sioux were on horses and made a grand entrance. They dismounted and formed a line to salute the Ojibways who had lined up for the ceremony. Governor Ramsey came with his interpreters and some other interested white observers. They took their seats and the chiefs of the two tribes placed themselves on each side.

The proceedings began with a speech from the governor that was both gentle and strong. He told them he had great respect for the brave warriors on both sides and wanted to count them as friends. He also made it clear that he could not put up with any more killings on either side and that they should all remember that the purpose of this meeting was to bring peace. After the governor's speech, a treaty made between the Sioux and Ojibway nations in 1843 was read aloud and explained. At this point, William Warren, spokesman for the Ojibways, rose to read a long statement in which he listed in detail the murders that had been committed by the Sioux. Then Bad Hail, the Sioux spokesman, made the same kind of statement, accusing the Ojibways of murdering Sioux Indians. At Governor Ramsey's suggestions, four white men were appointed, with the approval of the Sioux and the Ojibways, to decide what new agreement, if any, should be made. When all this was accomplished, the Indians adjourned this part of the meeting and prepared to hold their own council.

William had given much time and thought to the speech he gave at the council on behalf of his people. It was an honor for him to be asked to do this, for it showed that the Ojibways had great respect for his talent as a speaker and trust in his good judgment. They recognized that William was a worthy son of the crane clan. To do justice to his assignment, William had to know Ojibway history well so that he could give a true account of their suffering at the hands of the Sioux.

William stayed at the fort during the entire council, listening in on all the meetings and giving freely of his advice. He was pleased, too, at the final outcome. The Sioux and the Ojibway agreed that they did not need a new treaty. They informed the governor that they would abide by the old treaty and that he would have their support when he tried to enforce it in the future. The governor was very pleased by this decision and the following morning the proceedings were brought to an end with a great feast given by the opposing chiefs. The governor attended and gave each chief an ox as a present.

CHAPTER VIII

Elected
to the Legislature

In 1850 a great honor came to William Whipple Warren. In the fall of that year he was nominated and elected to be a member of the Territorial Legislature from the sixth district of Minnesota. Minnesota was not yet a state at this time. It had been organized as a Territory on June 1, 1849, and the first legislative session was called to order under Governor Ramsey on September 3 of that year, but it was not to become a state until 1858. William served in the second legislative session of Minnesota as the only Indian representative. The sixth district from which he was elected covered more than one-half the present area of the state.

He took his seat in Saint Paul as a member of the Territorial House of Representatives in January, 1851. The politicians, old and young, from all walks of life, were charmed by him. They referred to him as the "likable young Chippewa with the musical voice."

The Legislature at that time consisted of a House of Representatives and a nine-member Council. One of the first things that Governor Ramsey did was to call a joint session of the House and the Council on January 7 to hear his message. In his message the governor listed the items he thought would need their study and action during the session. He also made a strong appeal for a set of laws to govern the Minnesota Territory. Some of what the governor said was very hard for William Warren to understand or accept. The following is a quote from the actual text of the governor's speech.

> The memorial of the Legislative Assembly for the removal of the Chippewas from their ceded lands, was favorably considered by the President of the United States, who was pleased to instruct me to notify the tribe, that the privilege of hunting, fishing and gathering wild rice on lands, which had been sold to the United States would cease. The removal has not yet been entered upon, owing to the lateness of the day at which Congress made the necessary appropriation but the Indian Bureau will doubtless order the prompt prosecution of the movement early in the spring.

The governor also stated that he hoped the Senate of the United States would give them the right to take the Half Breed Lands on Lake Pepin so that a region rich in agricultural and mineral resources could be opened to industry. He then mentioned the Indian wars and the peace treaty that was settled in June of 1850. This was the treaty in which William had represented the Ojibway people and given their side in the arguments.

It is easy to see why William became angry at some of the things the governor said. William did not like the idea of moving the Indians to other land when he knew the Ojibways did not want to go. He remembered very

well the time he had led some of his people to Sandy
Lake for their yearly payment because the government
hoped they would like the country and want to live there.
They did not like it and did not want to live there. Also,
the fact that the President had instructed the governor
"to notify the tribe that the privilege of hunting, fishing
and gathering of wild rice would cease" must have
angered him. No one knew better than William that
hunting, fishing, and gathering wild rice were his people's
means of making a living. Even if they had sold their
lands, they should be allowed to keep the right to hunt,
fish, and gather wild rice from them. These rights should
not be allowed to slip from their hands because of a
treaty. How else would they live? Even as the governor
was reading his message many of the Ojibways were
starving in the cold of the winter.

The next day a letter from Hole-in-the-Day was read
to the Legislature.

> The undersigned, Head Chief of the Chippewa
> Nation, would respectfully invite the Governor
> and the Territorial Legislature of Minnesota, to
> be present at a representation to be made by
> him in behalf of his people, of the wrongs and
> sufferings endured by them.

> The meeting is to be held in the Presbyterian
> Church on Wednesday evening at half past six
> o'clock.

The letter was signed by Hole-in-the-Day, Head Chief.

Hole-in-the-Day was writing because his people asked
him to. It had been a long harsh winter for the Ojibways
and they were hoping against hope to get some help.

On the day that Hole-in-the-Day was to hold his meeting William was absent from the House of Representatives. He spent the day making sure everything was ready for the gathering at the Presbyterian Church. Since William was a Presbyterian himself he was in a position to help with the arrangements, and he felt responsible to see that everything went well at the meeting. Fortunately a large crowd showed up and Hole-in-the-Day made a rousing speech. He told them of the suffering condition of his people, how they did not have enough to eat or enough clothing to cover them from the cold. He pled for the needs of the Ojibways, and the crowd was moved by his speech. They appointed a committee to gather food, clothing, and money for their relief. But despite these efforts there was much hunger and sickness among the Ojibways that winter.

On January 9 the House of Representatives named the committees on which members were chosen to serve. William was fortunate to be assigned to the Committee for the Militia and the Committee on Territorial Affairs. Every affair that concerned Indians was assigned to the Committee on Territorial Affairs. This gave him an excellent opportunity to defend the rights of his people. Other members became familiar with William's voice as it was raised to protest some suggested invasion of Indian rights. Many of his fellow representatives, although they might not agree with him, had great admiration for him.

On January 15, the Legislature set to work in earnest to redo and change the laws of the Territory. In the original Act that established the Territorial Government of Minnesota, there were some parts that the Indian people strongly objected to. For example, the Act did not count Indians as part of the population when it decided representation. It also said that at the first election "every free white male inhabitant above the age of twenty-one years, who shall have been a resident of said Territory at the time of the passage of the act, shall be entitled to vote." This meant of course that the Indians were not allowed to vote. William was not able to get the Legislature to change this. As a matter of fact, it was not until 1868 that Indians were allowed to vote in Minnesota.

The work on establishing a code of laws for the Territory went slowly but steadily forward. William worked very hard on this, although health problems sometimes forced him to be absent. On March 31 the House adjourned. Its final act was the passing of a complete code of laws for the Territory of Minnesota. On this day the governor also approved the code and it became law. For a long time these laws were known as the "Code of 1851."

CHAPTER IX

William
as Writer

Many of the people who came to know William during the year he spent in the Legislature were impressed by his knowledge of Ojibway history and the many legends of the tribe. One of his admirers was Colonel D. A. Robertson, publisher of a Saint Paul newspaper called the *Minnesota Democrat*. Colonel Robertson was so impressed with William's knowledge and with his expressive and musical way of speaking, that he encouraged him to write down the stories and legends he told so well. William had always wanted to write the history of the Ojibways, so he began to make notes and write as fast as he could. Colonel Robertson agreed to publish what William wrote as a series of articles in the *Minnesota Democrat*. The first article was published on February 25, 1851, and was called "A Brief History of the Ojibways in Minnesota, As Obtained from Their Old Men." This was followed by other articles during the same year. Everyone who read what William wrote about the Ojibways seemed to find it interesting and many people wrote the paper to say so. Finally Colonel Robertson suggested that William take all the articles he had written, combine them with other material he had, and make a book out of them.

William liked this suggestion and began working very hard on his book. His health was not good at this time and he probably did not help it any by staying up late at night writing. But, by the winter of 1852, he managed to finish the book.

He was advised to get the book published in New York, so he set forth on the long trip. He also planned to see some doctors while he was in New York and perhaps get some new advice or medicine that would help his physical condition. The doctors in Minnesota had told him there was nothing more they could do for him.

The long journey held only sadness for William. The publishers in the big city told him they could put his work in print only if he provided the money it took to do so. William had almost no money at this time. His news from the doctors was no better. They said there was nothing they could do to help him and gave him no encouragement of ever getting better.

There was nothing for William to do but return home. His only hope was that, through the many friends he had in Minnesota who thought his writing was worthy of being made into a book, he might be able to raise enough money to have the book printed. But the return trip home was a difficult one and he became very ill on the way. He reached Saint Paul at the end of May, 1853, in a state of complete exhaustion. There he stayed at the house of his sister, Charlotte.

William thought he would rest for a day at his sister's home and then travel up the Mississippi back to the home he loved so much at Two Rivers. He missed his wife and

CHD 1186
.W294

May 11, 1853

Know all men by these presents that I William W
Warren of the County of Benton territory of
Minnessota am held and firmly bounded unto
William E Wickes and Timothy Lyons of the
City of New York and state New York, in the
penal sum of four hundred dollars, which
sum well and truly to be paid
      I bind myself, my heirs, executors
and administrators firmly by these presents
      The condition of the above obligation is such
that if the above bounden William W Warren
Shall procure or cause to be procured a good
and sufficient deed executed to William E Wickes
and Timothy Lyons of a quarter of a section
of government land lying in the county of
Benton territory of Minnessota and remit
the same to them within four months from date
Then this obligation to be null & void, otherwise
to remain in full force and virtue

Wm W Warren. (seal)

—New York.
May 11th 1853

*Bond of William W. Warren to W. Wickes
and Timothy Lyons for the location of
160 acres of land, New York, May 11, 1853.*

his family and longed to see the tall pines and the wilderness once again. But this was not to be so. On the morning of June 1 he began to bleed from his lungs, and in a short time he was dead. William was only twenty-eight years old — such a short lifetime to have accomplished so much.

His funeral took place the following day. He was laid to rest in the cemetery in Saint Paul. It seems a cruel stroke of fate that this man who loved the north country so much, whose heart was always with the clear streams, the wild flowers, and the whispering pines of the land of his people, was not buried there among the untouched beauty that had been his birthright.

William Warren's death brought sadness to many people. He had many friends who would miss him. He was mourned especially by the Ojibway people, whose voice he had been. He was their true friend, their brother. They were not to find another who would speak so well for them, understand them so truly, and love them so unselfishly.

The real tragedy of William's early death is that, of the wealth of information that was his, he was able to pass on only a small part to future generations. But William Whipple Warren is not forgotten. His book, *History of the Ojibways,* was published in 1885 by the Minnesota Historical Society, where some of his papers and notes are now kept. In 1957 a new edition of his book appeared, entitled *History of the Ojibway Nation* (Minneapolis, Ross & Haines, Inc.). So William's words live on, lasting reminders of the service and love he gave to his people, the Ojibways. To them his memory does not fade — it remains as clear as the call of the crane.

THE AUTHOR

Will Antell is the assistant commissioner
of education for the state of Minnesota.
Born on the White Earth Indian Reserva-
tion, Dr. Antell is a Chippewa of the
Mississippi band. Formerly director of
Indian education in Minnesota, Will
Antell went on to complete his doctorate
degree in education at the University of
Minnesota and then served for a year as a
visiting professor at Harvard University.
Dr. Antell has actively participated in a
number of community and professional
organizations. A past president of the
National Indian Education Association, he
is an acknowledged leader in his field.

*The photographs are reproduced through
the courtesy of the James Jerome Hill
Reference Library, Minneapolis Public
Library, Minnesota Historical Society, and
the State Historical Society of Wisconsin.*

OTHER BIOGRAPHIES
IN THIS SERIES ARE

William Beltz
Robert Bennett
Joseph Brant
Crazy Horse
Geronimo
LaDonna Harris
Oscar Howe
Chief Joseph
Maria Martinez
Billy Mills
George Morrison
Michael Naranjo
Osceola
Powhatan
Red Cloud
Sacajawea
Sequoyah
Sitting Bull
Maria Tallchief
Tecumseh
Jim Thorpe
Pablita Velarde
Annie Wauneka